D0065315

Published 2007 by
Zero To Ten Limited
Part of the Evans Publishing Group
2A Portman Mansions
Chiltern Street
London W1U 6NR

© 2007 Zero To Ten Limited
Text © 2007 Meg Clibbon
Illustrations © 2007 Lucy Clibbon

British Library Cataloguing in Publication Data
A catalogue record for this book is available from the British Library

ISBN-10: 1 84089 466 0
13 digit ISBN (from 1 January 2007): 978 1 84089 466 0

Printed in China

My Wicked Pirate Journal

from Peg Leg Meg
& Lucy Blackheart

A pirate is a robber who attacks other ships at sea.

January 1

Pirates all love a good party - and last night's was a big one. All pirates have a headache today.

January 2

January 3

January 4

January 5

Today's pirate phrase: **bilge rat**
A rat that lives in the worst place
on the ship, right at the bottom.
Not a nice name to call someone.

January 6

January 7

January 8

January 9

January 10

January 11

January 12

Today's pirate phrase: **keel haul**
Pulling someone under the bottom of the
ship to punish them. Hold your breath!

January 13

January 14

January 15

January 16

January 17

January 18

January 19

January 20

January 21

Pirate gear – **the cutlass**
This is a short curved sword for slashing at
enemies and slicing the tops off coconuts.

January 22

January 23

January 24

January 25

January 26

Today is Australia Day All pirates toss a shrimp on the barbie.

January 27

January 28

January 29

_____

_____

_____

_____

_____

_____

January 30

_____

_____

_____

January 31

_____

_____

_____

February 1

February 2

February 3

February 4

February 5

February 6

Pirate gear: **grog**
This is the strong rum that pirates
always drank.

February 7

February 8

February 9

February 10

In Malta, today is the Feast of
St. Paul's Shipwreck. Nobody likes
a shipwreck.

February 11

February 12

Pirate gear: **earrings**
Pirates love dressing up.
Some pirates thought that
heavy weights in their ears
would cure seasickness.

February 13

February 14

February 15

February 16

February 17

In the USA today is *Random Acts of Kindness Day.* All pirates know you have to be cruel to be kind.

February 18

February 19

February 20

February 21

February 22

February 23

February 24

February 25

Pirate places:
The Spanish Main
This was the area of South America from where Spanish fleets laden with treasure would set off for Europe. Pirates loved the place!

February 26

Pirate gear: **dubloons**
These were large gold coins that
pirates spent all their time trying
to find, or steal from one another.

February 27

February 28

March 1

St. David's Day
Welsh pirates check their ships for leeks.

March 2

March 3

March 4

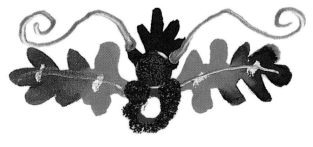

March 5

Pirate gear: **message in a bottle**
Messages were written on paper, rolled up and put in a sealed bottle. The bottle was then thrown into the sea in the hope that someone would find it.

March 6

March 7

March 8

March 9

March 10

March 11

March 12

March 13

March 14

March 15

March 16

March 17

St. Patrick's Day
St Patrick was a Briton captured by
Irish pirates and taken to Ireland as
a slave.

March 18

March 19

Pirate gear: **cat o' nine tails** The whip that ship's captains used on naughty seamen.

March 20

March 21

March 22

March 23

March 24

March 25

In Sweden today is Waffle Day!
Swedish pirates love a waffle.

March 26

Pirate gear: **the eyeglass**
This is another word for a telescope. Most pirates only had one eye, so binoculars would be no good.

March 27

March 28

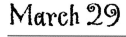

March 29

March 30

March 31

April 1

April Fool's Day. All pirates play
wicked tricks on one another.

April 2

April 3

On this day in 1880 the comic opera, *The Pirates of Penzance*, was first performed in London. It was about a group of gentle orphan pirates who aren't very dangerous. No real pirates attended the performance.

April 4

April 5

April 6

April 7

April 8

April 9

Annual 'Walk the plank' competition held at Tilbury Docks. Biggest splash wins.

April 10

April 11

April 12

April 13

April 14

April 15

Pirate food: **the ship's biscuit**
Biscuits lasted well so were
good to take on long journeys.
Even so they were often full of
maggots and weevils.

April 16

April 17

Pirate gear:
pieces of eight
Spanish silver dollars were sometimes cut into eight pieces for small change. Pirates didn't care – they liked all the money they could get.

April 18

April 19

April 20

April 21

April 22

April 23

St George's Day The day for English pirates to get misty eyed and think of home. Then forget it again.

April 24

April 25

April 26

April 27

April 28

Pirate gear – **treasure**
When pirates couldn't turn
treasure into money they
sometimes buried it. Then they
made maps so they could
remember where they left it.

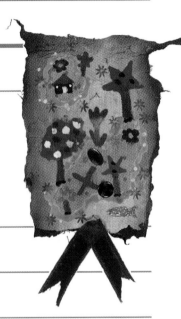

April 29

April 30

May 1

May 2

May 3

May 4

Pirate gear – **wooden legs**
Being a pirate was a dangerous business, and it was easy to lose a leg when everyone carried sharp swords.

May 5

May 6

May 7

May 8

May 9

May 10

May 11

Today's pirate word – **hornpipe**
The name of an instrument and
a dance – pirates just can't stop
themselves dancing.

May 12

May 13

May 14

May 15

A special pirate song:
Fifteen men on a dead man's chest,
Yo ho ho and a bottle of rum!
Drink and the devil had done for the rest,
Yo ho ho and a bottle of rum!

May 16

May 17

May 18

May 19

May 20

May 21

Pirate places – **the seven seas**
This means all the world's oceans.

May 22

May 23

May 24

May 25

May 26

May 27

May 28

May 29

May 30

May 31

June 1

International Children's Day
Pirates love children – on toast.

June 2

June 3

June 4

June 5

June 6

June 7

June 8

Today is **Bounty Day** on Norfolk Island, in the Pacific. Famous mutineers, led by Fletcher Christian, took over their ship and abandoned their captain, Captain Bligh, and some followers on a small boat, thousands of miles from land. Naughty!

June 9

June 10

June 11

June 12

June 13

Famous pirate:
Long John Silver
Not a real pirate, but a character
in *Treasure Island*, by Robert
Louis Stevenson. He had a
wooden leg and a parrot, and
was a mean and untrustworthy
rogue.

June 14

June 15

June 16

June 17

June 18

Pirate food – **small weevils**
Pirates always prefer small weevils over big ones, as everyone knows you should choose the lesser of two weevils.

June 19

June 20

June 21

June 22

June 23

June 24

June 25

June 26

June 27

June 28

June 29

Pirate word – **privateers**
Privateers were 'official' pirates who, using their own ships, were authorised by governments to attack and capture the ships of another country. One famous privateer was Sir Francis Drake.

June 30

July 1

July 2

July 3

July 4

July 5

July 6

Pirate gear: **the Jolly Roger** This is the name of the pirate flag used to frighten other sailors.

July 7

July 8

July 9

July 10

July 11

July 12

July 13

July 14

In France this is **Bastille Day**, when in 1789 the prison was stormed and all the prisoners were released. Hurrah!

July 15

July 16

July 17

Today is **Hurricane Supplication Day** in the US Virgin Islands. Please don't sink our ship!

July 18

July 19

July 20

July 21

July 22

July 23

Pirate gear: **hammocks**
Pirates slept in hammocks, and when they died, their bodies were sewn into their hammocks, weighted with cannon balls, and thrown into the sea.

July 24

July 25

July 26

July 27

July 28

July 29

July 30

July 31

August 1

Most French pirates take August
off as holiday.

August 2

August 3

August 4

August 5

Today's pirate word: **marooning**
This means leaving someone on a deserted island
to fend for themselves. Nice way to spend
a summer holiday!

August 6

August 7

August 8

August 9

Pirate word: **buccaneers**

These were pirates in the Caribbean, named after the French hunters that lived on some of the islands.

August 10

August 11

August 12

August 13

August 14

August 15

Famous pirate: **Anne Bonny**
Bonny was an Irish woman
who disguised herself as a
man to become a pirate.
She sailed with the pirate
captain, Calico Jack Rackham,
in the Caribbean, in the
eighteenth century.

August 16

August 17

August 18

August 19

August 20

August 21

August 22

August 23

August 24

Pirate gear: **tricorn hats**
These three cornered hats were very
popular in the eighteenth century.
Pirates wore them because they
wanted to look trendy.

August 25

August 26

August 27

August 28

Famous pirate: **Henry Morgan**
Morgan was a Welsh pirate who, after harassing the Spanish, was made Governor of Jamaica. He died on this day in 1688.

August 29

August 30

August 31

September 1

September 2

September 3

September 4

September 5

September 6

Pirate places: **the Caribbean**
This is the sea, full of beautiful islands, that pirates liked the most. Lots of ships to plunder, lots of islands to hide the treasure on, and palm trees to fall asleep under.

September 7

September 8

September 9

September 10

September 11

September 12

Pirate tip: scrape barnacles
off boots with a sharp cutlass

September 13

September 14

September 15

September 16

September 17

September 18

Respect for the Aged Day
Pirates are nice to their grandparents.

September 19

**International Talk
Like a Pirate Day**
Practise saying *'Arr!'*
and *'Run 'im through
with a cutlass!'*

September 20

September 21

September 22

September 23

September 24

September 25

September 26

Famous pirates: **Captain Hook**
Not a real pirate, but a character from Peter
Pan. Hook was Peter's enemy – Peter had cut
off Hook's hand and fed it to a crocodile.

September 27

September 28

September 29

September 30

October 1

October 2

October 3

October 4

In Sweden today is **National Cinnamon Bun Day**. All pirates love a good bun fight.

October 5

October 6

October 7

October 8

___

October 9

___

October 10

___

Pirate word: **Barbary pirates**
These pirates sailed out of North African ports in modern day Morocco and Tunisia, and would often capture Europeans and sell them as slaves.

October 11

October 12

October 13

October 14

October 15

October 16

October 17

Pirate gear: **eye patches**
Most pirate have eye patches.
This is because they forget
they have hooks, rub their
eyes when they get sleepy,
and lose an eye.

October 18

October 19

October 20

October 21

October 22

October 23

October 24

Famous pirate:
Barbarossa
Barbarossa, or
'Red Beard' was a
blood-thirsty
Barbary pirate in the
sixteenth century.
He was so successful
the Ottoman
Emperor made
him an admiral.

October 25

October 26

October 27

October 28

October 29

October 30

October 31

Hallowe'en!
The ghosts of dead pirates rise from the depths in the
night and frighten unwary sailors.

November 1

November 2

The Mexican Day of the Dead
Mexican pirates brag about how
many people they've killed.

November 3

November 4

November 5

Bonfire Night!
Fireworks, and the Guy getting burnt on the bonfire –
brilliant!

November 6

November 7

November 8

November 9

November 10

November 11

November 12

November 13

November 14

November 15

November 16

November 17

Famous pirates:
Calico Jack Rackham
Calico Jack died this day in 1720. He was the boyfriend of Ann Bonny, and spent many years fighting as a pirate in the Caribbean. He was eventually captured and hanged.

November 18

November 19

November 20

November 21

November 22

The day of Blackbeard's death

Blackbeard's real name was Edward Teach. He had a long black beard, carried knives and pistols, and was very cruel. He was killed by the Royal Navy in 1718.

November 23

November 24

November 25

November 26

November 27

November 28

November 29

November 30

Famous pirates: **the Vikings**
The Vikings were fierce raiders from Scandinavia that attacked and plundered European coasts from the ninth to the eleventh centuries. They used longboats with prows carved in the shape of terrible monsters.

December 1

December 2

December 3

December 4

December 5

Famous pirates: **the Ushkuiniks**
These were ruthless Russian river pirates that lived in the fourteenth century. They robbed and raided on the Volga, Ob and Kama rivers.

December 6

December 7

December 8

December 9

December 10

Famous pirates: **the Wokou**
The Wokou were Japanese pirates from the thirteenth century. They robbed, raided and smuggled along the coasts of China and Korea, and also caused trouble up the large rivers of China.

December 11

December 12

December 13

December 14

December 15

December 16

December 17

December 18

Modern pirates There are still many pirates on the seas, particularly in the Straits of Malacca, between Malaya and Sumatra. Pirates use speed boats to attack large ships, tie up the crew and then race off with the crew's belongings, or take the ship to a nearby port and sell its contents. Over a hundred attacks take place every year.

December 19

December 20

December 21

December 22

December 23

December 24

December 25

Christmas Day
Pirates swap stolen presents and
fall asleep in front of the television.

December 26

Boxing Day

December 27

December 28

December 29

December 30

December 31

New Year's Eve
The last day of the year. Have you run away to sea yet?